BLACK HISTORY MAKERS

Musicians

Debbie Foy

WAYLAND

Black History Makers: Musicians is an introduction to some of black music's most prominent singers, musicians and composers. These individuals have made styles of music that were once on the fringes of society accepted, and even revered, within the music industry.

However, the journey to success has not been easy. Getting paid, getting played and being appreciated was a constant struggle. There were tremendous barriers and prejudices; DJs unable to get air play, singers unable to perform in certain venues, choirs airbrushed out of history, recordings mysteriously disappearing... But despite these struggles, most people have given, and continue to give, an enormous amount of time, money and energy to charity. Like their music, the impact these individuals have had on the world will last for generations, making them true history makers.

So next time you hear that particular sound, whether it be soul, reggae or hip hop, know that someone, somewhere, at sometime fought for that beat, that right to be heard, so that you today can enjoy what is, in essence, the heartbeat of life — black music.

Remember, we got rhythm, we got class and we, in some instances, got recognised through this book at last.

Mia Morris OBE, Black History Month website

Published in 2013 by Wayland
Copyright © Wayland 2013

Wayland
Hachette Children's Books
338 Euston Road
London NW1 3BH

Wayland Australia
Level 17/207 Kent Street
Sydney, NSW 2000

Editor: Katie Woolley
Designer: Tim Mayer, MayerMedia
Consultant: Mia Morris, Black History Month website

British Library Cataloguing in Publication Data

Foy, Debbie.
  Musicians. -- (Black history makers)
  1. Musicians, Black--Biography--Juvenile literature.
  2. Musicians, Black--History--Juvenile literature.
  3. African American singers--Biography--Juvenile
  literature.
  I. Title II. Series
  780.8'996-dc22

ISBN: 978 0 7502 7875 1

Printed in China

10 9 8 7 6 5 4 3 2 1

Wayland is a division of Hachette Children's Books,
an Hachette UK company. www.hachette.co.uk

Picture acknowledgements
Jeff Albertson/Corbis: COVER, 15, James L. Amos/Corbis: 5
Bettmann/Corbis: 4, 6, Gareth Cattermole/Getty Images: 13
David Corio/Michael Ochs Archives/Getty Images: 3, 11
Joey Foley/FilmMagic/Getty Images: 17, William Gottlieb/Redferns/
Getty Images: 8, Douglas Kent Hall/ZUMA/Corbis: 22BC
Nils Jorgensen/Rex Features: 22TR, Georges de Keerle/Getty Images:
18-19, Tim Mosenfelder/Getty Images: 10, Michael Ochs Archives/
Corbis: 14, 18, 22BL, 22TC, 22TL, Pictorial Press/Alamy: 7,
Sasha/Getty: 9, Shutterstock: TP, 12, 16, 20, 21, 22BR

CONTENTS

Words in **bold** can be found
in the glossary on page 24.

What is Black Music?

In the seventeenth century, thousands of African people were sent around the world to work as slaves. Many were shipped to the United States of America (USA) to work as slaves on the cotton **plantations**. They brought with them songs and music styles from hundreds of ethnic groups across West Africa. These musical forms blended with other European influences and continued to evolve throughout the eighteenth and nineteenth centuries to form black music as we know it today.

When black people were transported from Africa to work on cotton plantations in the USA, they brought with them songs from many ethnic groups.

Early spiritual music

The slaves working on the plantations sang Negro spirituals – songs of **subversion** against their white slave masters. These songs formed the basis of a musical genre called the blues and later singers such as Paul Robeson (page 9) made their names singing this musical style.

The birth of jazz

Between the 1890s and 1920s, a style of music called jazz developed, created by black people in the southern states of Louisiana, Texas and Missouri, among others. Men such as Louis Armstrong (page 8) performed in large orchestra bands and as **segregation** was still in force, they often played to white-only audiences.

The 1950s and 1960s

During these decades, soul and **R&B** became a major influence, with singers like Shirley Bassey (page 12) becoming a legendary soul diva. Funk, said to have been invented by James Brown (page 10), was a blend of many sixties influences, including jazz and R&B.

The 1970s

The 1970s saw the invention of hip hop. Beginning at Harlem block parties, which were large public parties held in a neighbourhood, disc jockeys (DJs) spun records, most typically funk, while masters of ceremonies (MCs) began improvising over the top with lyrics or 'raps'. This musical style gave rise to talents such as Jazzie B (page 22) and later Jay-Z (page 20) and Alicia Keys (page 22). At the same time, **reggae** became a musical force and a focus of **black consciousness**, thanks to artists such as Bob Marley (page 14).

Harlem block parties of the 1970s were usually large, outdoor community gatherings, from which rap music emerged.

Pop and crossover

In the 1980s and 1990s, black pop and R&B artists such as Michael Jackson (page 18) and Beyoncé (page 21) sang a type of pop dance-soul that became phenomenally popular. These pop '**crossover**' success stories paved the way for many other artists, both black and white.

Over four centuries, the music of African Americans has largely dominated the musical landscape. Black music has often grown out of slavery, poverty, struggle and religious belief. In this book we explore how the diverse musical styles of today have been influenced by the legendary black musical history makers of the past.

Samuel Coleridge Taylor
Composer & Activist

Samuel was born in London and brought up by his mother and grandfather, who was a professional musician. At the age of 15, he won a scholarship to study violin and composition at the Royal College of Music in London. He married in 1899 and, in spite of objections towards their mixed race marriage, the couple had a son, Hiawatha and a daughter, Gwendolyn.

Taking America

Backed by the famous composer Edward Elgar, by 1896 Samuel had earned himself a reputation in musical composition. His success led to a tour of the USA in 1904. It was there that he began to take an interest in his cultural heritage and in black **activism**. His aim was to incorporate African music into his compositions. Greatly admired by African Americans, Samuel was named 'the African **Mahler**' on a trip to New York in 1910 when he was invited to the White House by then US President Theodore Roosevelt.

Shy composer

Though he was a shy man, while he conducted an orchestra Samuel was a great communicator and his hugely successful *Hiawatha's Wedding Feast* established him as one of Britain's outstanding composers. However, he earned little money and he had to teach and conduct to make a living.

Name: Samuel Coleridge Taylor

Born: 15 August 1875, London, UK

Died: 1 September 1912

Musical talent: Composition

Interesting fact: He was named after the famous poet, Samuel Taylor Coleridge.

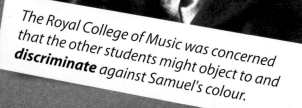

The Royal College of Music was concerned that the other students might object to and **discriminate** against Samuel's colour.

Though little of Samuel's music is available today in printed form, Hiawatha's Wedding Feast was described as 'one of the most remarkable events in modern English musical history' when it was first performed in 1898.

His campaign

In Britain, he suffered **racist** attitudes and remained, until his death, a strong supporter of the Pan African movement, which called for the empowerment of black people throughout the world. He died of pneumonia at the age of 37, but his two children, Hiawatha and Gwendolyn, carried on in the family tradition, becoming well-known conductors and composers.

MAKING HISTORY

During Victorian Britain, black people found it difficult, if not impossible, to achieve recognition for their cultural talents. The black classical composer Samuel Coleridge Taylor was one of the first to help break this mould, paving the way for many other black people to gain recognition for their musical talents.

Louis Armstrong

Founding Father of Jazz

Name: Louis Daniel Armstrong

Born: 4 August 1901, New Orleans, USA

Died: 6 July 1971

Musical talents: Jazz trumpet and cornet, and singing

Interesting fact: The Federal Bureau of Investigation (FBI) kept a file on Louis regarding his outspoken views on **racial integration.**

Louis Armstrong's pioneering musical style had an impact on many millions of future musicians.

Born into a poor Louisiana family, Louis Armstrong grew up in the care of his mother and grandmother, rarely seeing his father. From the age of seven, he worked various jobs to help his family financially. One of those jobs was to carry coal to the entertainment district of New Orleans, where he would stand outside the dance halls and listen to the bands playing inside.

On the Mississippi

Louis grew up singing in the streets for money and playing the cornet in local bands. In his early twenties, Louis also worked the riverboats of New Orleans on the Mississippi River. He was one of the first jazz men to play trumpet solos and combine singing and **scatting** in his performances.

Speaking out

Louis had strong views on racial integration, some of which were explored in songs, such as (What Did I Do To Be So) Black and Blue? During the Little Rock Crisis of 1957 in which the government prevented nine black students from entering Little Rock High School, Louis cancelled a tour of the Soviet Union, claiming publicly, 'the way the government are treating my people in the South, they can go to hell!'

Louis Armstrong died of a heart attack at the age of 69, but his pioneering musical style and strongly held views on racial integration have had an impact on many millions of people.

Paul Robeson
Singer, Actor & Activist

Early years

Paul was the youngst of five children in the Robeson family. At the age of six, Paul's mother died in a house fire and his father lost his job, so the family relocated to Somerville, New Jersey, USA.

Great talent

At his new school, Paul was talented in the classroom, on the stage and on the sports field. Paul graduated from university with top grades and moved to New York to study law. He worked as a lawyer while singing and acting in his free time.

Spreading the word

In 1928, Paul starred in a London production of the musical 'Show Boat' and his career took off. In spite of his popularity, Paul had to deal with racism and from the mid-1940s, he devoted himself to political causes.

In 1949, Paul toured Europe to speak out against the discrimination of black Americans. After some of his appearances ended in riots the US government refused to allow him to travel abroad, so he toured the USA encouraging black people to fight for their rights.

Charismatic man

Paul Robeson was an outspoken man who used his position in the limelight to fight injustice and try to bring about social change.

Name: Paul Leroy Robeson

Born: 9 April, 1898, Princeton, New Jersey, USA

Died: 23 January, 1976

Musical talent: singing

Interesting fact: Paul sent his nine-year-old son to school in the Soviet Union to avoid the racism Paul had suffered at school.

Paul Robeson was an athlete, actor, singer, academic, author and vocal political activist.

James Brown
The Godfather of Soul

James was known as 'the hardest working man in showbusiness' because of his drive and limitless energy.

Name: James Joseph Brown Junior

Born: 3 May 1933, Barnwell, South Carolina, USA

Died: 25 December 2006

Musical talent: singing, songwriting, keyboards and guitar

Interesting fact: As a young child, James was so poor that one day his school sent him home for having 'insufficient clothes'. This may explain why in later life, James loved to dress elaborately.

Early influences

James's parents divorced when he was five, so he was raised mainly by his great-aunt. Growing up during the **Great Depression** of the 1930s and in the segregated Southern states, James faced extreme poverty and racial discrimination. He learned to play the drums and guitar and was influenced by watching gospel preachers scream, dance and fall to their knees during sermons.

First recording

At the age of 15, James was arrested for breaking into cars and ended up at reform school, where he formed a gospel group. He later joined an R&B band called The Flames and, in 1956, they produced their first recording *Please, Please, Please*. The track sold three million copies and launched James's musical career.

The 1960s and 1970s

In the 1960s, James's music was often associated with black **nationalist** movements and tracks such as *Say It Loud – I'm Black and Proud* (1968)

James Brown was renowned for his exciting and exhilarating stage shows that were feats of precise timing and great stamina!

were seen as a way of calming political and racial unrest in some American cities.

In the 1970s, his songs featured on the sound tracks for the popular '**blaxploitation**' films *Black Caesar* (1973) and *Slaughter's Big Rip-Off* (1974).

The later years

When hip hop emerged in the 1980s, DJs and songwriters frequently sampled Brown's songs on their tracks and James Brown continued to be known by a new generation as the 'Godfather of Soul'.

James's life was beset by problems including the death of his wife, drug use and ill-health. He died at the age of 73. His elaborate memorial service involved a golden casket and videos of his concert performances.

MAKING HISTORY

James Brown was one of the most influential figures in twentieth century music. Renowned for his vocal 'screams', his feverish dance moves and his extravagant sense of style, James Brown put the notion of 'rhythm' on the pop musical map and played a major part in the development of soul and funk.

Shirley Bassey
The Original 'Bond Girl'

Shirley's big voice and love of glamorous clothes and jewellery marks her out as a performer who loves to put on a show!

Name: Dame Shirley Veronica Bassey

Born: 8 January 1937, Cardiff, Wales, UK

Musical talents: singing

Interesting fact: Shirley Bassey is often affectionately nicknamed Burly Chassis, in reference to her powerful voice and lungs.

In October 1964, Shirley topped the charts in the UK and US with *Goldfinger*, the theme to the James Bond film. She followed with several other hits in the 1960s, including the enormously successful *Big Spender* (1967).

Beginnings

Shirley was the seventh child of Nigerian parents. She left school at the age of 15 to work in a factory and sang in pubs and clubs in the evenings and weekends. She was discovered by a bandleader, Jack Hylton and in 1955, she left Cardiff for the 'bright lights' of London. Just two years later, Shirley had a top 10 hit with her first single, *The Banana Boat Song* (1957).

James Bond

Goldfinger led to two further Bond theme collaborations: *Diamonds Are Forever* (1972) and *Moonraker* (1979). During the 1980s, she fell out of the public eye but in 1997, on the eve of her sixtieth birthday, she came back in true 'Bassey style' collaborating on a new album with the band, Propellerheads. The album *History Repeating*, attracted a whole new generation of dance fans and brought Shirley back into the limelight.

Later success

Shirley's reign as the Welsh diva of the music industry has lasted for five decades. With a love of glamour and her trademark powerful voice, she has enjoyed one of the longest chart careers in British history. To top a distinguished career in showbusiness, she became *Dame* Shirley Bassey in 2000.

Dame Shirley wows the audience at the BBC's Electric Proms festival in 2009.

Bob Marley
Reggae Hero

Name: Robert (Bob) Nesta Marley

Born: 6 February 1945, Saint Ann, Jamaica

Died: 11 May 1981

Musical talent: Singing and songwriting of reggae and ska music

Interesting fact: His song lyrics are often highly political, including the words of Haile Selassie, the twentieth century Ethiopian emperor and key figure in the Rastafarian movement.

Through his music Bob Marley helped to spread the word of the Rastafarian movement to a worldwide audience.

Rural childhood

The son of a black teenage mother and an older, white father, Bob spent his childhood growing up in a village in Jamaica. With his friend Bunny Livingston (later known as 'Bunny Wailer'), he learned the guitar and practised his singing skills.

Big break

In the late 1950s, he moved to Kingston, living in one of the poorest areas of the city. Bob formed a band called the Wailing Wailers in the 1960s, and while they had some success in Jamaica, the band found it difficult to make money. But, in 1972, they landed a record contract and success soon followed.

In 1974, a track on their *Catch a Fire* album entitled *I Shot the Sheriff* was covered by Eric Clapton. It became a number one hit in the USA, putting the re-named Bob Marley & The Wailers on the musical map.

Reggae superstar

The band toured the world, spreading the word on reggae. In the UK, they had their first top 40 hit with *No Woman, No Cry* (1975).

During the late 1970s, Bob became an international music superstar. But his fame and nationalist beliefs made him a target for people who were opposed to his ideas and after a failed **assassination** attempt in Jamaica in 1976, Bob fled to London.

Last years

The band travelled to Africa and played at the independence ceremony for Zimbabwe in 1980. They had planned a tour of the USA to promote the album *Uprising* (1980) but were stopped when Bob became ill with cancer. Just before his death at the age of 36, he received the Order of Merit from the Jamaican government. Adored by Jamaicans, he was given a hero's burial.

Bob Marley is often remembered for his protest songs in support of social revolution, but he also released many gentle, soothing love songs.

> " I don't stand for the black man's side; I don't stand for the white man's side. I stand for God's side. "

Bob Marley

MAKING HISTORY

Bob Marley is credited with being the world ambassador for reggae and a key figure in the Rastafarian ('rasta') movement, which drew its beliefs from many sources. He was also one of the first international superstars to come from a so-called 'developing world' country.

Stevie Wonder
The Singer with a Vision

Stevie was born six weeks premature and was blind from birth. Nevertheless, his parents were determined Stevie would live a normal childhood and they encouraged his love of music from an early age. He was a member of the church choir and played a number of instruments including the piano, harmonica, drums and bass.

First recording

At just 11 years old, the talented youngster impressed Berry Gordy, the owner of Motown Records in Detroit, the highest-profile black-owned record label in America. Working under the name 'Little Stevie Wonder', Stevie released two albums in 1962 and had a number one hit in the US pop and R&B charts with a song called *Fingertips (Pt 2)* in 1963.

Social activist

Stevie's music had much in common with the civil rights movement's desire for integration and a better deal for the black working man and woman. His classic recordings from the late 1960s through to the late 1970s such as *Living For The City* (1973) dealt with poverty and racial tension. The number one single *You Haven't Done Nothin'* (1974) was a protest song against the disgraced US President, Richard Nixon, who was forced to resign over the **Watergate Scandal** in 1974.

Name: Stevland Hardaway Judkins

Born: 13 May 1950, Saginaw, Michigan, USA

Musical talent: singing, songwriting and keyboards

Interesting fact: Stevie's 1980 single, *Happy Birthday* was part of a successful campaign to make civil rights campaigner Martin Luther King's birthday into a national holiday.

Stevie believes his loss of sight gave him a heightened awareness of sound.

A wider audience

Determined that his message should be heard outside the narrow black R&B market, Stevie toured America supporting rock group The Rolling Stones, and recorded with pop artists including ex-Beatle Paul McCartney and Elton John.

Stevie has recorded over 30 US top 10 hits, and received 22 Grammy Awards. He is still performing today and visited the UK in the summer of 2010 for a series of concerts.

Stevie performs in support of Barack Obama at a presidential campaign in Indiana, USA, 2008.

MAKING HISTORY

In 2009, Stevie was named a United Nations Messenger of Peace, having been recognised as 'an artist who used his voice and special relationship with the public to defend civil and human rights and to improve the lives of those less fortunate.'

Michael Jackson

The King of Pop

Name: Michael Joseph Jackson

Born: 29 August 1958, Indiana, USA

Died: 25 June 2009

Musical talent: singing and songwriting

Interesting fact: Michael had a short marriage to Elvis Presley's daughter, Lisa Marie Presley, from 1996 until 1998.

Michael Jackson was born into an African American working class family, the youngest of five brothers. Their father, Joseph, believed his sons had talent and so shaped them into the musical group, The Jackson 5. Michael was just five years old when he joined the group.

Chart toppers

When the band signed to the famous Motown label in 1968, Joseph Jackson became their manager and pushed his sons to spend endless hours rehearsing. The group went on to have

Michael's stage presence at such a young age meant that he soon became the lead vocalist and dancer of The Jackson 5.

many hit singles including *ABC* and *I'll Be There*. From the age of 13, Michael launched his solo career and in 1972, had his first solo number one single, *Ben*.

Moving on

The Jackson 5 cut their ties with the Motown label in the mid-1970s and signed a new recording deal with Epic Records. Michael soon emerged as a talented songwriter and working with legendary producer Quincy Jones, released his hugely successful 1979 solo album *Off The Wall.*

But it was Michael's next solo album *Thriller* (1982) that sealed his legendary status. The album produced seven top 10 hits and launched the famous dance, the 'moonwalk'. The video for *Thriller* was a high-budget affair with stunning special effects and the single stayed in the charts for 80 weeks.

Aid in Africa

His next two albums *Bad* (1987) and *Dangerous* (1991) were successful, but not on the scale of *Thriller*. During the 1980s and 1990s, Michael worked on several humanitarian projects including USA for Africa's 'We Are The World', which raised funds for the poor in Africa.

Final years

From the early '90s onwards, his private life made the headlines and by the 2000s his eccentricity began to overshadow his musical talent. A planned comeback tour in 2009 never got off the ground as Michael suffered a heart attack at his home in Los Angeles, USA and died at the age of 50.

Michael performs on stage at Wembley Stadium, London, UK, during his BAD tour, 1988.

MAKING HISTORY

Michael Jackson was the best-selling black music artist of all time. He was also regarded as one of the most talented, gifted and eccentric performers we have ever known. His enormous 'crossover' success in music and dance (including the highly popular 'moonwalk') has led to a generation of musicians who are influenced by him, such as Whitney Houston and Justin Timberlake.

Jay-Z
Hip Hop Entrepreneur

Name: Shawn Corey Carter

Born: 4 December 1969, Brooklyn, New York, USA

Musical talent: Rapping

Interesting fact: Jay-Z took his name from the 'J' and 'Z' subway trains that ran through the Marcy Projects, the housing estate where he grew up.

Jay-Z's performance style is smooth and slick and relies on clever wordplay.

Shawn Corey Carter grew up in a single-parent home in the Marcy Projects, Brooklyn, New York, USA. Shawn sold drugs as a teenager but turned to rap as his ticket to a better life.

Early business venture

With two friends, Jay-Z started up a record company called Roc-A-Fella and not long after he released his first, self-financed record *Reasonable Doubt*. But it was his 1996 release called *Ain't no Nigga* that catapulted Jay-Z to fame.

Jay-Z effect

Before long, Jay-Z had changed rap from a music style that sensationalised violence to a new style of rap that celebrated high-end clothing, expensive cars, jewellery and fine champagne.

Rap entrepreneur

Jay-Z continued to produce best-selling albums, such as the Grammy Award winning *Vol.2 Hard Knock Life* (1998) and *The Blueprint 3* (2010), featuring his successful *New York State of Mind*, which was number one on the Billboard Hot 100 for five consecutive weeks. But it is his interest in the business side of the music industry which sets him apart and he is one of the most financially successful rap artists in the world.

Jay-Z has made millions from his business ventures. In 2008, he married Beyoncé, one of the most successful pop artists of all time. Jay-Z is fast becoming a modern music legend.

Beyoncé
The R&B Sensation

Name: Beyoncé Giselle Knowles

Born: 4 September 1981, Houston, Texas, USA

Musical talent: singing and songwriting

Interesting fact: Beyoncé sang at both of President Obama's inauguration ceremonies.

The daughter of an African American father and a Creole mother, Beyoncé attended singing, ballet and jazz dance classes from a very early age.

Forming Destiny's Child

By eight years old, she was a member of an all-girl group, Girl's Tyme, that eventually became Destiny's Child. In 1997 the band, managed by Beyoncé's father Matthew, signed to Columbia Records. Destiny's Child went on to sell over 20 million albums, with strong female-centric hits including *Independent Woman Part 1* and *Survivor* (2001).

Going solo

By 2003, all of the band members had moved into solo projects and Beyoncé released *Dangerously In Love*. The five-million selling album had two hit singles, including *Crazy In Love*, a collaboration with her now-husband, rapper Jay-Z, and started her on the path to phenomenal solo success.

Social conscience

Beyoncé has long supported social causes. With Destiny's Child bandmate Kelly Rowland, she founded the Survivor Foundation, to provide housing for the victims of Hurricane Katrina in 2005. She also supported World Children's Day and Hope for Haiti in 2010.

To watch Beyoncé live in concert is to be amazed by her energy, dance routines and spectacular stage shows!

MAKING HISTORY

Beyoncé holds the record for the most musical Grammy Awards won in one night – six! She is ranked by *Forbes* magazine as the most powerful and influential musician in the world.

Other Music Heroes

'Duke' Ellington (1899–1974)

This jazz band leader and composer was born in Washington DC, USA. He wrote his first composition before he had even learned to read music. In 1923, he moved to New York and was a regular performer at the famous jazz venue, the Cotton Club. In 1969, President Nixon threw a party at the White House to celebrate the 70th birthday of this great musical legend.

Nat King Cole (1919–1965)

A jazz pianist, songwriter and vocalist Nathaniel was taught music by his mother. In 1939 he formed the King Cole Trio and toured Europe, playing in front of the future Queen Elizabeth II. His future wife Maria's parents did not support her decision to marry Nat, claiming he was 'too black'. However, in 1948 they were married. He made many successful TV appearances before he died of lung cancer at the age of 46.

Jazzie B (1963–)

This DJ, rapper and songwriter was born in London, UK. With producer Nellee Hooper, they formed a musical collective called Soul II Soul, which went on to be one of the most innovative dance/R&B outfits of the 1980s. In 2008, he was awarded an OBE and the Ivor Novello award for being 'the man who gave black British music a soul of its own'.

Ella Fitzgerald (1917–1996)

As a 16 year old, jazz singer Ella won first prize in a singing competition in New York. She joined a band called the Savoy Swing Orchestra and, in 1938, she made her first record. Four years later she launched her solo singing career and went on to become known as 'The First Lady of Jazz'.

Jimi Hendrix (1942–1970)

This rock guitarist and singer was born in Seattle, USA. He played the guitar from childhood and, in 1966, came to England and formed a band, The Jimi Hendrix Experience. An exciting performer, Jimi soon gained a wild reputation. But his lifestyle began to cause him problems and he died a drug-related death at just 28.

Alicia Keys (1981–)

This R&B and hip hop artist was born in New York, USA. Her musical talent began to emerge at a very early age, taking piano lessons from the age of five. She began to practise her songwriting skills in her early teens. Her musical influences while growing up were diverse, ranging from rappers Biggie Smalls and Tupac Shakur, to jazz musicians Miles Davis and Nina Simone, to Stevie Wonder.

Timeline

Legacy

1875 Samuel Coleridge Taylor is born

1901 Louis Armstrong is born

1920s Jazz music reaches its hey-day

1928 Paul Robeson shoots to fame appearing in 'Show boat' on the West End stage

1933 James Brown is born

1929–1930s The era of the Great Depression begins in 1929 after the Wall Street Crash and lasts for many years

1950 Stevie Wonder is born

1956 James Brown's first record *Please, Please, Please* with his band The Flames sells 3 million copies

1964 The James Bond theme *Goldfinger* bcomes a number 1 success in the UK and USA for Shirley Bassey

1968 The Jackson 5 signs to the Motown label

1976 Bob Marley flees to London after a failed assassination attempt in Jamaica at the Smile Jamaica concert in Kingston

1982 The release of Michael Jackson's *Thriller* album becomes the biggest-selling album of all time

2003 Jay-Z and Beyoncé collaborate on the single *Crazy in Love*

2008 Beyoncé and Jay-Z are married

2009 Michael Jackson dies

The legacies of the musicians in this book live on, not only in their achievements but also through the work of their families, friends and followers:

http://www.
thesurvivorfoundation.com/
Beyoncé and former Destiny's Child bandmate Kelly Rowland set up the Survivor Foundation to provide help for victims of disasters, including housing for victims of Hurricane Katrina in 2005.

http://www.bobmarley-
foundation.com/foundation.
html
The Bob Marley Foundation was set up in 1986 and continues to support communities in need across the world.

http://jamesbrownfamilyfdn.
org/site
The Brown Family Children Foundation began in 2007 to continue a legacy started by James Brown, who set up projects to help underprivileged children and impoverished families.

Glossary

Activism To take direct action (such as a protest or demonstration) to achieve a goal.

Assassination To murder a prominent figure.

Black consciousness A movement seeking to unite black people and take pride in the black race.

Blaxploitation The word is a mix of 'black' and 'exploitation'. Films featuring black actors. They were designed to appeal to a black audience.

Crossover This refers to a black artist who has success appealing to a majority white audience.

Discrimination The unfair treatment of a group or person, based on their race.

Great Depression A period during the 1930s when there was a worldwide economic depression.

Mahler Gustav Mahler (1860–1911) was a famous Austrian composer and one of the leading conductors of his time.

Nationalist Somebody who supports the independence of a country or people.

Plantation A large estate or farm where crops are grown and tended to by workers.

Racial integration To join races together.

Racism Abusive behaviour towards another race.

R&B A style of music mixing rhythm and blues.

Rastafarian movement A form of religion that originated in Jamaica and regards the Emperor of Ethiopia (Haile Selassie or 'Ras Tafari') as God.

Reggae A style of music, originating in Jamaica.

Scatting Jazz singing that uses vocal sounds instead of words.

Segregation To be set apart from a main group.

Ska A fast style of music with a strong off beat, which originated in Jamaica.

Subversion To act against a governing power or authority.

Watergate Scandal A 1970s political scandal in the USA which led to the resignation of the President of the United States, Richard Nixon, on August 9, 1974.

Index